P9-EDR-062

SOMETHING
SWIMS
OUT

Since his work first broke into the open, Darrell Gray has consistently penetrated to the crux of matter, shedding light on everything in between.

With this book he puts us precisely in touch with that method of reality where all is in a constant state & constantly moving.

This touch, these poems, generate an energy which carries the self through language and beyond. Nothing is lost, though, for poetry, like perception, is most itself when it is continually going beyond itself -- into the infinite alternate lives and their objects, where a single syllable can remodel the future.

SOMETHING
SWIMS
OUT

DARRELL GRAY

SOMETHING
SWIMS
OUT

BLUE WIND PRESS : IOWA CITY

Grateful acknowledgment is made to the following magazines
in which some of these poems first appeared: Kayak, Poetry
(Chicago), Poetry Northwest, The North Stone Review, The
World, Gum, Kamadhenu, Doones, The Hospital Quarterly,
The Iowa Defender, Intro 2, Painted Horses, Golden Arches,
Search For Tomorrow, and Planet News.

The poems "The Excuses," "A Tone Diverts The Summer,"
"The Dream Wedding," and "Presence" first appeared in
EXCUSES (Abraxas Press, 1969).

The author wishes to express his gratitude to the U.S. De-
partment of Agriculture for a generous grant of foodstamps
without which this book would not have appeared.

ISBN: 0-912652-01-2 (woodbound, signed)
       0-912652-02-0 (softbound)

Collages by:
Tim Hildebrand (pp. 20, 43, 59, 68
George Mattingly (36, 49, 73, 81
Darrell Gray (pg. 87

Back cover photo: Tim Hildebrand
Front cover: George Mattingly

issued as Search For Tomorrow Special Number A

contents

All these years I have not had to remember these things. They have remembered themselves.

Black Elk

TO THE READER

The reason you have been placed at the edge of this ocean is to increase you in directions hitherto not known. There are many things for you to learn. As April is closing in on an ancient heel, sparks fly off, and these rudimentary passions will lead you to a new discovery, buried and smiling — a knowledge which in the total energy of its cities distracts from love as love distracts from savagery its balanced thunder. The grass, for instance, has begun to grow more quickly now that the sea has expanded its base of reference — doors in the cities appear to be opened less often. Everything now participates in how even the birds suspend their resistence, and the landscape projects its original metallic cry.

This cry is heard in three distinct and coexistent aspects : *coming, going,* and their hybrid which prevents our extended notice, as on a trajectory one can say "Hi" to whatever form approaches — perhaps a girl coming down to the beach for a swim, separate from the sun, in the amazing context that has formed to contain her, merging at last with the white ambience of the waves.

So you see, though the scene includes a great many automatic and penetratingly shaky elements, it cannot be reduced beyond the assumptions that give it birth, even as you yourself cannot choose not to be there, cloud-like, poised in a process completing itself at a distant point you call your *life,* sloping stones down to the water; thunder inside; light some years away.

TODAY IS WATER

Today is water
flowing from the faucet.

I shave, noticing a smear
the rain left on the window.

Outside, dark pools
are lying on the ground.

Leaving the house,
I see myself in the water,

smaller in the smallness
of the pool.

THE VISIT

the angel of
dust
came by this morning

he wore
a cape of
old stars

in his eyes
I saw
the glacier
move

he said nothing
and that
was enough

SONNET

after Supervielle

That we may not forever be alone
All objects sing in silent inhuman voices
Through the room where we sleep, flesh
To flesh. . . .and the trees run deeply
As we turn. My hand falling over
Your shoulder consists of spaces,
Darkness like the ground. In dreams
The animals return. The tiger sees in us
A tiger, and the snake a snake. Each one
Recognizes in us his brother,
And the bee gives us a sign
To fly away with her, and the hare
That he knows a hiding place hollowed
In the earth where you cannot die.

THE LIGHT IS NOT WRONG

The light is not wrong
to have covered so simply

the one downcurving branch
so late in the evening

POEM

The stones have come so far they cannot speak.

PRONGS

The prongs of graphite and leather.
The prongs of shoes reflecting the moon.
The prongs of watermelons at a picnic.
The delicate prongs of icicles.

The prongs of justice and the prongs of lice.
American prongs and the prongs on incubators.
The prongs asleep in the eyes of turtles.
The prongs that shiver like hair.

Black prongs.
Red prongs.
The prongs of arthritic barbers.
The prongs beneath seats at cheap theaters.

The prongs of feminine recognition.

MOVING

There comes the time
    moving its house,
the yard and cat
    that can't come back.

The dark was big. The car
    went through,
And what they thought
    they thought they knew ---

the yard, the house,
    the car, the cat.
Goodbye, goodbye. It
    seemed so real.

WHO

Who
is this
mouth
like pain
in soft
places --
anger tearing
the words
into
time.
In
the body
no
need to
stand
still,
as
light
waits
in the
face like
a cave
of
Goodbye.

THE ATTACK OF THE FIFTY-FOOT HERSHEY BAR

As if to prove the ending can be sweet
wrapped in raging cellophane
it comes --

its rumble shaking us
into belief, greater than Godzilla
or Rodan.

Red and wild, we run
down streets we thought we understood.
Some jump in cellars

reeking of dead rats, light up
their broken cigarettes
and pray

the army's on its way, that bombs
can kill this monster
that grew too big to love.

COMING BACK

She comes back
    in his mind, among
the cats & green
    sprigs of flower,
the room suddenly
    more than
a joining of walls.
    She touches glass,
moving her night
    along the backs
of chairs, curves
    of her hair
like the sound of
    a door left open.
But it is not
    enough,
the touch, the turning,
    the moon --
light falling
    through its own
white body, come back
    to the dark-
ness it loves.

THE PLACE

I stood
by the door
thinking

I could
be standing
by the window.

Then I
would be
over there,

not here,
and would see
things differently.

So move away,
I think, to
where I'm not,

and break the place
by doing what
I thought.

WITH MY MOUTH THAT IS
WARM WITH DISTANT LIGHTS

With my mouth that is warm with distant lights
with my mouth of darkness & the whirr of bees
with my mouth of infinity covered by the slanting snow
with my mouth of sweet rockets & rivers of crumbling
      umbrellas
with my mouth like an anvil composed of the essence of
      zip codes
with my mouth like a point of view
with my mouth like an incandescent escalator on which a
      brown toad falls asleep & dreams of two planets col-
      liding
with my mouth like Iowa covered by the shadow of a bird
with my mouth like the end of a Russian novel
with my mouth of thick prose little branches cubes & stairways
with my mouth of old echoes & turbulent hidden arrivals
with my mouth of the motion of plants bedrooms wet dreams
      & stars
with my mouth arriving late at the birthday of desire
with my mouth full of accidental wings & bridges
with my cobalt mouth in the late-afternoon of the mailbox
with my mouth containing teeth & a tongue & convolutions
      whirling inward to the brink of hazy beams
with my mouth of the sex of grapes moving over a breast of
      exciting dimensions
with my mouth suspended in the window of a passing bus
with my mouth in which poems wake up & shoot out without
      shattering
with my mouth that never knows it is a mouth
with my mouth like the unfolding of the instant
      a puzzle that once put together will creep away

with my mouth of the Gold Coast white waves & ships in the
        distance
I breathe & sing, prolonged by the sway
        of everything coming & going at once

                                                    13:vii:70

ZOO BABIES

Relieving its desperate clumsiness
The concentration of monkeys has risen from time
To time

Once, in a zoo at night I saw them crawling simply
Like future events previously unnoticed
Tho held in an awkward position for so long
They sag with potential logic

The leathery ears protruded, masculine and cold
Or feminine and warm, I don't know which

Later I took an enormous bath
Without an appreciable notion
Of how desire dissolves

Waving its furry claws in all directions

THE EXIT

You are now approaching
the exit. The door
is marked by a green

light saying itself,
but the door may be small,
may be a flame

running up a wall, or
fall at your feet,
flashing. Things change

so often here that no
one knows how to breathe
in the proper manner,

but you, in your bombproof
skintight pants, living,
as it were, on the edge,

look cool and at ease.
But when you get to the door
it gets to you. You see

yourself out there,
surrounded, thinking
Flame, cool Flame, oh flashing.

TOUCHING THE WINDOW

". . the buried stream
That nourishes the known."
---Richard Wilbur

Touching the window,
it touches you back. The hills
don't break when the flattened tip

of the finger follows
their lines, and distance
presses on the eyes. Blood

doesn't wake the glass
if you shove your hand
through the window. There's

no one at home in the clouds,
although sometimes you see
what seems a face ---

dark eye, nose, and lip.
Here, you listen like a flame
and almost hear the earth

working to make a good cliff,
a better wing for the next
born bird. And all the while,

the mirror stays on the wall,
showing a spider on the clock
until it webs the hanging

room, and you turn
to what's there. Outside,
the sky goes on for miles.

FOR THE FUTURE OCCUPANTS

Having shortened the space between our fingers,
and felt the walls pull finally apart,
we are no longer ourselves

on edges, nor care to be.
Breaking the surface of the formal past
we discover endless cups of coffee,

paper-weights containing tiny oceans,
and old shoes emitting a slow
blue light.

Our neighbors in the bone stand close together.
Their children draw on our doors
mountains and rivers,

and below them, in bold letters:
IF THOSE THINGS IN THE DISTANCE ARE STARS
THEY'LL HAVE TO BE TAKEN AWAY

No one listens to the shafts of sunlight
arriving continually to take our place.
At the moment, we are not here. The moment is

shortening, taking us
in. But we come back on the sand,
on lawns. We look around.

We are on an archery range that extends forever
like a photo of arrows caught in mid-flight.
Some of us have glimpsed the dart-games of ruminant angels,

and some, touching the delicate curves
of clavicles, have forgotten their names.
We are going back to where we had no name,

back through the grass, through the groves
of pianos. We are approaching woodlarks, crickets,
and bridges long covered with water.

In the distance, transparent tractors
climb the terraced hills, and into the fields of dark poppies
whose seeds contain old photos of the Civil War.

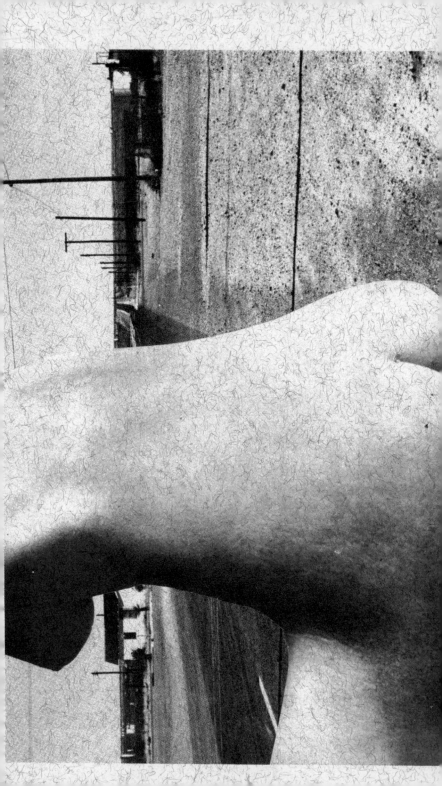

PLANETS
for Cindy

Our bodies are like the shadows of unborn planets.
Sometimes, when we are alone, they are all we have.

INDIVIDUALS ARE SOMETIMES FOUND

Individuals are sometimes found
at noon on patios sighing.
Whatever the wind was, surely
it meant them no harm. A
parachute unfurls in the
foreground; water-towers
are resembled into sleep.

A single ray keeps returning
into the whorl. This is the
world in which what is separate
falls short at the movies,
drives home through the frost,
remembers. An individual

heliocentric dog. Two wounds
striking light in a petal
that whirls through TV, ends
in not beginning: a vision of
chairs in its place, chosen
with blue proclivities, pride

in replaceable vases. Once you
were there, and it became time,
especially receptive to the growth
of pleasure and the strange
interior children. A tone away.
Compressed around the heart,
compact and shining, the new
day's ambiguous crystals.

THE THOUGHT

When I think of everything I have been thinking
It appears like the reflection of footprints on a glass floor
Through which I look down on the park
Containing the bodies of the young girls
Under the trees, their faces startled by the glass
Birds flying through the green depths of the day --
Typographical errors take root, and the future becomes
An enormous glass harp attracting the sleep of animals
As my life continues to roll its electric ball of darkness
Leaving no mark on the ground.

ELEPHANTS

"Elephants are at home anywhere."
—Peter Schjeldahl

1

How can we sleep with all these elephants
Around us? Oh Muse, must I placate you
Like the moon! I'm not so young anymore,
And moonlight on those huge sad humps
Leaves me helpless. Must they stand
At the foot of our bed? My peanuts are gone,
And their trunks are cold and hard.

2

Remember the jungle? Of course. Let's go
To sleep. I can't. Those mounds of sunlight
Running all over our feet. We were lost
For days in the wind. When miracles
Fell on us we had forgotten their language.
It was like living in a cloud. We felt
A breeze and suddenly the ocean appeared
"Out there," or so we said. I had a toothache.
You photographed the local ferns and vines.

3

It was there we saw the elephants. They
Were walking on the water, their long tails
Leaving little waves behind them. It was beautiful ---
Those huge things silently on the water.
When we left, they followed. Now, our house
Is a heaven of snorts. The yard looks tough
In the sun. We live somehow, loving
And helpless, and always in their shadow.

PRESENCE

The door was a "jar"
in a field of space
controlling the night
in Ohio. And it was
all there: the voices
reproduced as violets
in the book beside you,
the fruit lit up with a strange
precision --- each contour
inventing your life.

SOMETHING SWIMS OUT

Something collides with something
and the luggage explodes in Utah

Something opens a capsule of seeds
causing the boat to arrive at the beach

Then something grows large in a church-bell
until white hands extinguish the candles

Something is spilled over the gowns
at the Rainbow Gallery
while outside, the pear trees
are found to contain
small porcelain pellets
that fall, one at a time,
into the dewy grass

Something carries an armchair into the sky
while something else assembles rockets
in a field near the tear-shaped air-base

On the coast of Madagascar
a huge steel tube protrudes into the ocean
from the far end of which, just before daybreak,
something swims out

AND

And is a willow cheek hurried by yellow spokes.
It speaks of a great confusion gently lifted.
*

Accidents, while glowing on its peaks, do not derange us:
The monk said "and" and uncovered a meadow of claws.
*

In the "and-light" a tiny ape
can make an alarming difference!
*

Mistaken for an ant, it lay buried,
and then it shot forth like a star. . .
*

The sheet of paper contained the imprint of a giant mammal.
And was the ears and eyes.
*

And is the pain in cosmology.
*

And is the gas station of the Infinite.
It moves and includes all distance.
*

And buds.
*

And is a trinity of little curves and wishes.
*

Near the foxglove, a tiny though turbulent "and"
resumes like the head of a child.

*

Open the window? An "and" might leap on the arm.
*

In the igloo, a small pile of "ands" lay shining
with enormous effort.
*

The sunlight hits you. So does "and" in a crisis.
*

Inside the rose it is different.
A conjunction of darkness moves like a lacework of "ands."
*

And, being feminine, sleeps among waves and worlds.

YOU

. . .It was meeting you, in things
That brought us out, to touch
The edge: a darkness made
Of all the light there is. The clouds,
Though chilled with their impractical
Events, have entered as memory's

Steep chime among yielding nodules.
The way back is now not anything
Like a gravel playground; the new
Victories of sunlight, growing
Oblique, have been placed in their proper
Boxes where they can vibrate

As loud as they like without
Disturbing us with needs or
Damaged eagles. The only cure it seems
Is to reject the metaphysics
Of medicine entirely, and plunge
Ahead, partial, while staying put.

These differences are not
Our total feature, for we can be
Ourselves and never know it, though
Harmlessly arranged in fields
Or valleys, sending out messages
Whose only source we always thought was you.

SONNET

The great wish into which we look
Its mouth concentric like a tourist's
Is merely the analog of accidental choice
In which imagination and beauty meet
And fly off into deeper hair-do's, like
The insect's editorial against an anxious thigh
You meet while casually crossing the street

The next person you know will always remember
How the grace was allowed to filter through a shrug
Instead of, wing-like, changing the whole affair,
While feelings were penetrating a spherical sense
Which was "you." The fountain overflows.
Like "fangs," the drops roll, till they sound like
"Thanks," and fall to the green intensity of the grass.

A SITTING DUCK

However far you have come the direction changes
And there are no clear ideas, not even of day
In which the most real is but a form of forgetfulness
Sending its beams far apart. In the newspaper

A particular branch had broken: the lawn around it
Was prevented into sprinklers through the use
Of clouds. The stairway was burnished pine for awhile, and
It rose like a figure of speech to its destination: translucent

Lips. Once at the beginning of Spring you had thought
That near the end of the night the stars would gather,
Not so much to listen to blood flowing in the veins, no,
Not interruptions, leaves on blue sound, or the ruffled

Mind in which these things don't end. It is *thought*,
You think, and what you don't know can't hurt you.
Still, it's hard to tell where the edge is. The broken
Blade of the lawnmower, an interrupted sweetness, closing

Again. This accumulation startles you, and yet is the essence
Of peace, of the seasons at peace in their mild reversals,
The actual branch with its stranded centerless buds, in the
Night which has come to mean for you, descending and
                                        rising at once.

from THE ORIOLES

Traveling develops these emotions
placed to reflect obliquely on themselves. . .
Stepping off the porch in the rain
or sunlight, the inconsistencies bearing their small
yellow leaves along the moment's garage.
                                    Turbulence.
                                            A cup
held so that it does not fall. Toward us
the turret moves, and down its expanding nozzle
the universe creeps and is vital.
                            The words
are formed on a tray under the slow-moving light
of the elm.
            You move your lips.
                            And it is Sunday
asleep on the styrofoam mattress, hair
deepening the area around you.
                            The lightbeams
intrude on a bowl. Perhaps the importance of this
will leave to compose another intricate image
where purpose fails to ignite it. Hugs
are intense displacements. In our minds, in
our hearts, we love the formations of bodies.
If that were not so, how could we endure this consciousness
which seems always to be taking us away.

The fiend stands behind the fire and is no longer destroyed.

He is in love with the little leaps that collide,
interlacings of light
and darkness, coeval precisions of gold.

In his life the lightwaves nudge at the cells
where isomers lie coiled in the heated darkness,
shifting their minute hairless anatomies, like stars.

This structure extends to where you cannot see.
The letters lie on the table,
their messages vibrating softly
as if under water. You cross the room
and the whorl deepens.

                         Outside, in the lot facing
the house, a new building is irregular —
an example of how we can look
at the twentieth century, while once
we were young in the distance.
You were a small
girl then, you were very young.
You were holding the photo of the orioles
that I remember you loved — the blue
small bodies of the birds borne upward
away from the sacrifice you could not imagine.
So there are things that must go unimagined,
for they are the perfect spheres of preserved emotions,
the open field between the trees where the young girl walks
in a dream of many small blossoms.
                         It is hard to remember
how the hands in their unconscious search
divide the warm grasses
on the hill where her mother
lies buried, her heart like a secret star
succumbed to the calculus of dew.

The choice of these words is not another matter.

In the morning, we cannot avoid
the painful impressions left
by the newscast as it flashed
the poor progress of peacetalks.
The voice in our room
has reminded us — a static of sunlight
replacing what we would have otherwise said.
The generations move. They make no sound.
My mouth at the small of your back
where the moist hair quivers in the air
that has come over farms in the night
bearing the pollen and the cries of the orioles
that can assuage our grief.
                              In the act of,
the space belonging to the poem, I trust
that these words carry their meanings
as you carry what cannot be held forever
into the world.

POEM

*"grace to be born and live as
variously as possible"*
—Frank O'Hara

I

The lightning arranges us
here in the tranquil reaches
where the red flowers
have history to grow from.
Around them, we become
direct & conversational,
having stood for so long
accomplishing great stumps
on the frozen lawn. But soon
we imagine, we will collide
with furry places — the rose's
moist explosion — symmetrical,
dangling, alert.

II

One cannot close this eye.
For it is the world in the end
that moves us — its miraculous urges
waking us each morning. The sky
focuses on all the strange little plants,
and we are among them, strangely,
holding a cup of coffee,
because we can't be perfect.
And the car drives over it,
soundlessly, its volume equivalent
to the air its movement displaces.

THE TIMES OF DAY

Make love in the
Blue rooms

The yellow
And bronze

The fluttering white
Curtains in the

Green yellow pale

Make the small
Hands do

Music
In time

On the flesh-
Colored flesh in

The sunlight

THE EXCUSES

Excuse me for the hips
I barely know them
And the bones — candle-shaped
And burning in the window
You forgot to close
Or fog

Excuse the burdens
Sifting down out of my
Headache colored photo
Of the lot — your tennis
Shoes haven't showed up
Through the decades
Of the hardly noticed
Mountains, real as pop

And excuse those terrible
Shiny warts in the grammar
I never use — My name
Or the name of the
Bullets someone shot
Your father with,
Coming to life

To excuse new chemicals
With sleep, I smoked
All through that movie
Of the lips and streets
Starring Cary Grant who said
Excuse me to Alexis
Smith, you're lovely

A TONE DIVERTS THE SUMMER

The lights are a risk in the unconscious effort
One thinks of their movement
As mutable tables are covered with tiny wings
In rooms reproduced on the hillside

A girl with the gaze of an angel
Today might not be invisible
When the lightning unfastens its silvery bone
And the moment becomes a system of docks and tears

The tables support an effort of mutable risks
The lights flow over the flesh
The wings reproduce a silence over the docks
As a bedroom appears in the morning

THE DREAM WEDDING

Pressure gets in the eye.
Its pain is round.
During the lapse of several years
Would you care to smuggle this strange little plant?
By the small unbearable noiseless sleeve
Just after the porch those lovers visit ---
I dig persistent holes in the leeway
To improve their seasonal drift.
Out of that wind, tho, flashlights keep us awake.
You get up and swell the oysters with a lovely color,
Say, of the sky, or that dangerous beach-colored breeze
Falling expensively over the wedding
Of dreams. So soon they assume
That even penmanship outlives them,
There in the imprecision of their huts
Reflected like a drawing on the water.
A lampshade covers the feet and ankles of the swimmer
Tho, in a potentially emblematic disaster,
While you and I play on the smuggled guitar
As if nothing happened. Steam rises,
Which is really a hurt form of water,
Into the air that is really
Rising to cloud. And I wonder who,
In all these relationships flickering on and off
Will find our tears grown shiny and strange with pressure
Here in the only world we know or love.

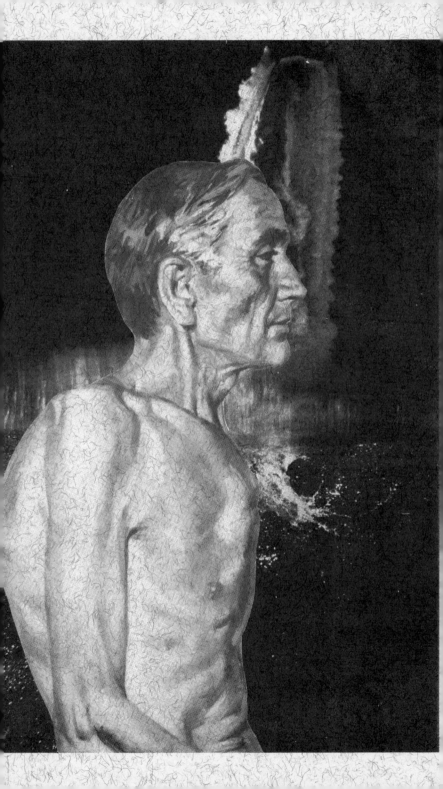

POEM FOR THE NEW YEAR 1970

A thin copper wire leads the light to this place

Eternal Hum
of the pinecone

Globe Hum / Space Nipple of your sister sunlight   Oh

opening my eyes

to survey the immediate

configuration of

"news"

The Halo

circling the hole   fear   Bed

An elegance prolonging shapes   No

Desk-top strewn with
various direct &
indirect objects

Three green Galo wine-bottles

from the past

Ashtray

full of places   (ashes?)

man
u
scripts

can-opener

THE NATION
35¢

Polyethelene container containing the Absence of
LUCERNE PASTEURIZED DELUXE ORANGE SHERBERT

                      the sky continuous between

         NESCAFE COFFEE &

    Mama Cass

On my new sly-rug a small bug opens its wings again
To test the air for messages &
Moving nodes

               Look! there goes a node now

     expanding the MATCH COVER which sez

    INCREASE YOUR EARNING POWER FAST!

(past increases flower. . .)

             A "strike-over"

             voice

          on the air

Just like Pope   winged goofballs in the reddish night

                          splat!

         smile

            (some static)

Its time to give birth to poems   mirrors   clouds

         Letters from
              Jim Humphrey
              George Mattingly
              Dave Drum
                  & Ray

all to be answered soon
from new constellations
under the same
but clearer moon

SPACE

filling the room

(Where's Keats?)   too full to not move   slide   sway

arrange

. . . The process of smoking Peach Blend tobacco in the dark

glow of the radio

And down the hall

a frenzied female scream

(Murder? Orgasm? Epiphany?

I guess I'll never know.   Such

is the nature of life in this

Cosmic Hotel

—banana peels

Toothache

EXCEDRIN / Midnight

Its the NEW YEAR!

Happy for That!

Oakland
2:i:70

GAS STATION

Something is being filled. A part of everything is filling something else. When whatever is waiting is full, it pulls away, leaving us standing here in the glow of the vapor.

THE POEM MACHINE

This is a sky machine,
mostly beneath which

the day machine
and the shadow machines

come forward to the you-machine.
The eye machine

records the mist machines
entangled in the tree machines,

releasing twig machine
by twig machine

the small dew machines
that fall on the black

insect machines
beneath. The cloud machines

darken, are closing now against
the spongy hill machines

in the distance machine,
while in the house machines,

the people machines
slip into the sleep machines,

their love machines silently
running.

SONNET

Beyond the immediate sensation lies a sea of light
Where the objects of passion exist in their purest essence
So as not to obstruct each other, or the passage of love.
A fullness, unnumbered, and wholly beyond us
As we move through this or that city, oblivious
Even to the world in which our feelings lie immersed,
Though what is only real can become much more.
You may want to carry something out of all this nuance,
A sort of memento of past resilience, in whose heart
You divined new temperatures, thoughts, and connections
Between even the fruit and the sunlight dividing attention.
On the beach, for instance, you felt unique and happy
Though alone, as though another world within this one
Of water, trees, birds, and their impressions, appeared
As you saw in the passive shallows the wet shells shining.

THE MOST EXCITING CENTURIES

The most exciting centuries will always pass by
Like beautiful girls in t-shirts

SUMMER ACID: A COME-DOWN, WITH MUSIC, TWO BEAUTIFUL GIRLS

You and she and it in the room with
the music surrounding
such forms as the mind makes---people
talking, in the spaces they
bring, laugh

ing in one
form of the same over-
lapping life.

She says she is
alive, and throws
out her arms, love-

ly, oh
so small &
dark against the white

morning sky.

VAPOR LOCK

Wasn't there some other moment, then?

We saw you start

a nuance, making something from wood

that landed.

But soon it turned into a "problem," a sort of continual

fixation on the landscape, table-legs emerging

incomplete, to distribute the sky

into equal zones

for the impression of birds & jets.

No feeling is greater than this.   Though stones

remain under water,

we can easily see them.

And the white clouds filling

the sky at this moment

their light-filled isolation like a sea

whose slightest whisp receives a strict attention

before it becomes just another beautiful vapor

in the thousand parts of the day

5:vii:70

BRAIN DAMAGE

Since prose you ran between the lines
stunned into sadness & those vans like secret blooms
taking away all "fixtures"

Still
    there are sensitive cones in the landscape
Digestion construes the tenor   He is a part of you, hence
the bee´s broken wing, the shoreline. . .

                  It rains here only a
little roof that we show
with moving disbelief
to the captives—
the pain around the pump, the glands, and stars.
It takes us back along the line of trees: flash-
light: new form of conduction: kiss

         flesh/light further in the book

that would merely be a *fact*
were it not for the lotus-shaped holes it makes, here,
in the sunlight shifting an arm through the surface, or tears.

Such lifting bends even prose

while clams accrue
like syllables of the sea

and asteroids suspend the facial gestures.

A STONE

Lifting it up,
it rushes away
to the other end
of its song.

COLORADO SPACE SONNET

for George

In Colorado, midnight, I am thinking
in
    Colorado, smoking, that
how the sky, everything, darkens,
          purposefully, at

. . .nothing "on."   Yes, that's *it*, in
the sky, writing, my desk overpiled with falling
Life. The moon is both new &
included in the poem of my chair.
          The air,
               in Colorado,
thinks like trees. A breeze can be
alone as often as,
          smoking,
              I rise
turn up the radio, the moon, SWEET STEEL,
in Colorado the night writing
Angel, asleep & slumping in the
               space chair,
      warm wine in the clear, green glass.

27:v:70
Boulder

COLORADO SPACE SONNET 3

Up all night again, where space is singing, here
in Boulder in my head & tongue. "In the mountains
there you feel free." T.S. Eliot said that. He
knew a lot about things, I guess, tho I have always
secretly hated THE WASTE LAND. What point is there
in telling everyone how shitty things are? They must
find this out for themselves, no? Actually, things
are totally great! The ground is flowing through
the night, with plant-like ornaments, and stars. I read
poems by Samuel Beckett (POEMS IN ENGLISH), Ted's
SONNETS, and *Elm Fuck Poem* by Ed Sanders. I know
what he means. "A whistle blows shrilly." Outside
the window the street ends in a (pill). I take that pill
& am gone. Birds fly because they have more imagination.

COLORADO SPACE SONNET 5

Its 4:13 AM Friday morning, May 29th
& I have just finished a Torpedo sandwich. I think
about George in Iowa City, Dave in Madison, and Merrill's
new book, TRUCK, which hasn't arrived. Space filled with
"tendencies," a rising light. In a hotel the world is quiet. No one
is walking, nor are they heavy, nor do they snore. A camel's
back, trusting. The first car goes by---a little dull roar
of gas. This is not really a poem. My stomach growls
in its sleep, trying hard to digest the things I
give it. Do eyes "digest" the objects they perceive?
Does the mind eat? I am obsessed by the inconstant
universe: my poems are probably problems, not *proofs*.
Just now I belched. Lewis MacAdams writes his poems in
the nude. Had T.S. Eliot done that, no doubt he would have
                        written a hell of a lot fewer poems.

3 JULY 1971

the flower, Jane, you mailed to me
was wilted to some degree

tho when i put it in a glass
dimensions to the world came back

and i slept easily
within the body of the night
which was a ring of endless light

which was a ring of endless light

POEM

A simple verticality
Sustains us. We are contained
Like the lake-light, on small rocks

       ---Look, everything changes

Strange angels swerve in the dew.

ULTIMATE THINGS

The face of the ape
is its sense of separation.
Wherever we travel, its into
that fur, those eyes.
Reading, walking, listening,
each separate act a
form of what grace is
allowed us, and between us—
the experience of the beautiful
failures: *intention*
making a world.

SCATTERED BRAINS

The reason for everything fills an invisible room
I'm in that room now
It's like a one-way bird with clear blue wings
A little loud and shivery at the edges

Someone comes in

Not Allan
Not Cinda

It's the other me
Writing
the other "you"

CHRISTOPHER COLUMBUS

The small dark speck on his eye was a distant ape.

MENTAL BODIES ENFOLDED
IN PHYSICAL WAVES

Beyond the interval, a rest overtakes it. We think of eating again. An image becomes an implement while its opposite sails off, confusing the neighborhood's negative space. Still, there are things which fit nowhere. Reality like the imprint of a sneeze.

Another sneeze and you are miles away, being born or just rushing up a flight of stairs. The stairs are constructed from the gaps in consciousness, sunlight falling on the steps in waves, while the woman at the top of the stairs sings in a darkness seemed to be made of light—a mental body enfolded in physical waves.

The interval recurrs, intact like the scream of a toad in the moist vegetation of memory.

THERE IS AN INFINITE SILENCE
AT THE CENTER OF THINGS

What
　　　did we say
that we thought
we had said,

the mind so turned
and was in view.
I sat

on the narrow
bed with
things before me,
trying to see.

If we go there,
(I think), the park
will be green, continuous
flakes from the

statue's eyes, cars
like a form of memory,
almost a song. But

the street is
something else, or
not there---hung
in the mind like

an arm's reflection,
coeval and afraid.

BAFFLING TURNS

asleep at 60 mph

ULTIMATE THINGS *part 2*

In the wilds of the Universe
an orange popsicle is melting.
Time comes to this, wakes up, and

brushes its teeth. Real hens
exhibit their mysteries openly,
as if they were rarely situated

within a pen. Moons pass over
the distance; wafers and bars.
Captivity obeys the balanced sphere

beyond its true expansion. The girl
in whose mind this has all been
happening has long since left,

because of the caves in her
development, and because what
she thought she thought came true.

LOVE POEM

I have given you my nights,
my fever and its stars,
the comets that come
only once
through the day that breaks to reclaim
division, green mountains
under the snow
when the music stops
and a feather of landslides erases the tear in the curtain,
the existence of the world
resulting in shudders,
entrances & wars
swallowed up by the shaking translucent
center

a name that had to be stolen from the sheer cascade
of lips at a picnic
the shifting of tiny nights at the core

and now, "ashtray,"
you say as you lift it, all the weight
of what you remember to know, not to slip off
into abstraction, & the cigarette
burning through both worlds, both rooms of the thought
as love projects us into its intricate prism

one word foreshadowing the many swerves of
the sun
passing itself in our hearts

Boulder
30.x.70

POEM FOR THE NEW YEAR

The ends of the sun
are reflected, and in our lives
become the birds you see, walking
home late through the snow,
carrying a sack of groceries
because on earth love weighs
like a can of soup, canteloupes, & lettuce
grown between the sun and what
you cannot think to say.

                              1 : 1 : 71
                              iowa city

90

This book printed in the United Space of America & available from Blue Wind Press, Box 1189, Iowa City, Iowa 52240.
Designed, laid out & type set in Perpetua & IBM Press Roman by George Mattingly. Printed at Diversified Press & ECI, Coralville, Iowa, in an edition of 1500 softbound copies & 100 woodbound copies, of which 26 are numbered a-z and signed by the author.

Darrell Gray was born and raised in
1945 in Kansas and California. He
has been an encyclopedia salesman,
gravedigger, high school "substitute"
and part-time carwrecker. Mr. Gray
has been to school & is the editor
of the post-futurist magazine, *Suction*.
He appears all over, and lives and
works in Iowa City, Iowa.

Darrell Gray